How to Stop Overthinking

Declutter Your Mind with 8 Proven Strategies to Stop Negative Thinking, End Anxiety, and Overcome Worrying.

By

Jake Trevor

Copyright © 2020 – Jake Trevor
All rights reserved

No part of this publication may be reproduced, distributed, or transmitted in any form or by any means, including photocopying, recording, or other electronic or mechanical methods, without the prior written permission of the publisher, except in the case of brief quotations embodied in reviews and certain other non-commercial uses permitted by copyright law.

Disclaimer

This publication is designed to provide competent and reliable information regarding the subject matter covered. However, the views expressed in this publication are those of the author alone, and should not be taken as expert instruction or professional advice. The reader is responsible for his or her own actions.

The author hereby disclaims any responsibility or liability whatsoever that is incurred from the use or application of the contents of this publication by the purchaser or reader.

Table of Contents

Introduction 6

Section I 13

Introduction to Overthinking and Its Effect on Your Life ... 13

Chapter 1 14

Getting Started 14

    How Our Brain Works When We Overthink 16

    What Overthinking Is and Is Not 18

    Causes of Overthinking 22

    Signs of Overthinking 26

    Effects of Overthinking 28

Chapter 2 31

Anxiety, Negative Thoughts, and Worry 31

    What Triggers These Thoughts? 31

    Write Them Down in a Journal 39

    Why You Should Write Them Down 41

Section II 48

Strategies To Stop Overthinking 48

Chapter 3 49

Ending Negativity and Embracing Positivity 49

    Reflect on the Bright Side of Life Everyday 49

    Live in the Present 56

    Change the Way You Think: Gratitude Vs. Regret 61

    Act with Confidence 62

Chapter 4 67

Create a To-Do List 67

    How Your Life would be Without a To-Do List 68

    How a To-Do List Helps with Overthinking 71

    Maintain a To-Do List & Stick to it 72

    Creating an Effective To-Do List 76

Chapter 5 82

Live a Minimalistic Lifestyle 82

    What is Minimalism? 83

Benefits of a Minimalist Lifestyle 84

How to Live a Minimalistic Lifestyle 88

Chapter 6 95

Get Rid of the Past and Bad Relationships 95

Get Unstuck from Your Ugly Memories 96

Let Go of Certain People 103

Tips to Shake Off Bad Relationships from Your Life...... 105

Chapter 7 111

Pursue your Goals 111

Discover Your Vocation 113

What Motivates You? – Your Passions 117

The Goals That Work - S M A R T Goals 119

How to Set SMART Goals That WORKS!..................... 122

Chapter 8 126

Practice Mindfulness 126

What is Mindfulness?... 128

Why You Need to Practice Mindfulness 129

Effective Techniques for Practicing Mindfulness 130

    Mindful Meditation 131
    Mindful Observation 132
    Mindful Listening and Breathing 133
    Guided Meditation 136
    Reflect on Your Thoughts 137
    Self-Compassion Breaks 138

Chapter 9 141

Be Happy 141

    Live Your Best Life 142

    Steps You Can Take to be Happy 144

Chapter 10 148

Reach Out to Someone 148

    Get Professional Help If All Else Fails 149

Conclusion 151

References 153

Introduction

Are you like this?

Meet Charles.

Charles is an optimistic young man with all the visions and bright hopes of changing the world. For a long time, he has known that he is talented in the fields of negotiation, people management, and emotional intelligence. Coupled with that is the knowledge that he would make a great business person.

He knows this because many people have told him so at various points in his life, and he also has those moments when he cannot but think of himself leading a foremost tech industry and being the agent of change he so desperately wants to be.

For a while, Charles has harbored the thoughts of setting up a business to start offering the solutions he wants to offer at a global level. He needs to start testing out all that he knows, meeting new people and making new connections, and he also needs to start learning how the market operates and the principles the industry runs on. At the back of his mind, Charles knows that the financial independence he seeks, and the opportunity to make the lives of people easier with his skills and business idea, all lie in his execution of the first step, which is to start putting structures in place.

He sees it in his dreams; he is called to be much more and do much more than the 8-6 he is currently working, and there is no way for him to achieve all he wants to if he does not begin somewhere.

The desire to step up is burning brighter in Charles's mind, and there is nothing he can do except to take the first step. So, he decides to meditate a bit to gain some clarity - and this is where the interesting things begin to happen.

During those few minutes, he takes out to think on some things, Charles cannot stop his mind from drifting a bit too far away from the agenda he has at hand. He goes in with the idea that he was going to gain clarity and find the strength to take the first step he needs to take in the direction of the actualization of his dreams, but...

Doubts are beginning to creep in. Now that he is thinking about it, Charles can see the loopholes in his business idea. These loopholes seem to be too big that he cannot help but scoff at the thought that he was going to set up a business in the face of these apparent questions.

Where are clients going to come from?

How am I sure that I will be able to break free of the competition in the market and brand my business in such a way that attracts the attention of the clientele I want to work with?

How am I going to be able to do that and still be effective as a paid employee of another organization?

His business idea begins to seem ridiculous to him. Big tech companies are in business; Microsoft, Apple Inc, Google, and their network of tech solutions, and all the rest of them. Doubts about how he is going to set up a business in the face of these giants and still succeed begin to nibble away in his mind. As the seconds keep ticking away, the voices at the back of his mind keep increasing in intensity. These voices are telling him to give up the ridiculous idea and focus on the 8-6 he currently has; after all, a lot of people are looking for what he is looking to throw away on the grounds of a ridiculous idea.

Snapping out of the meditation time, Charles gets up from where he is seated, looking defeated. There is a slump in his shoulders and a droop in his posture that can only be the result of an internal dialogue that did not quite turn out right. Just like that, he gives up on his dream of contributing his quota to the advancement of the society, and goes back to live in his mediocre life; all because the second option presents him with some form of comfort and safety, while the first option demands that he be a bit reckless and challenge his comfort zone.

Back to the question asked in the first line of this book.

Are you like Charles?

No, you may not be in the process of starting up a tech

company (or any company at all), but you may be on the verge of doing something worthwhile with your life. You have made all your plans, and you are brimming with excitement. You believe your idea is great, will be very helpful to the advancement of the society, and will serve a lot of good to you as the plan begins to unfold. You are happy, until...

The little voice at the back of your mind begins to whisper funny things to you.

You begin to question the validity and potentials of the ideas in your mind. You begin to scoff at your own ideas, and you discover that the energies you have gathered before (that were supposed to be channeled towards the actualization of your goals) begin to dwindle.

You are overthinking it, and the more you do, the worse it gets. The more you do, the more ridiculous your ideas begin to seem to you. Your anxiety levels are rising, and you are beginning to feel too pessimistic. There is a peg that has been placed on your productivity and your ability to reach out to the better version of you that awaits. Before you know what is happening, you let go and give up on the amazing dreams you had, the visions you saw yourself achieving, and the goals you were about to meet. All because you were not able to let go of the reins of your mind and stop overthinking things for a minute.

Here's the truth; the more you keep overthinking things, the less productive you will be, and the less you would tend to love yourself. It is a simple compound effect thing, and you must be able to stop the cycle from the beginning; stop overthinking things. This is what this book is here to help you with.

This book is a guide. It is a blueprint that takes you on a journey from the person who overthinks everything (and is not able to do much because he spends all the time and energy he should be spending on execution, worrying over ways in which things could go wrong), to the person who is bold, courageous and able to take the first step toward the actualization of his goal (notwithstanding how bleak the road may seem).

Consider this to be a roadmap that will take you

through a series of 8 proven strategies that have worked for countless people over the years. If you are able to read, assimilate and apply all that you will learn in this book, you will see that by the time you are done with the last page, you would have encountered a clear path to get you to stop negative thinking, end anxiety, and overcome excessive worrying.

This way, you will be more equipped to become the person you want to be, live the life of your dreams, and achieve all that your mind sets to achieve. The key to living the dream life you want to live lies in this book.

You are ready for the journey, aren't you?

Without further ado, let's jump right into it.

Section I

Introduction to Overthinking and Its Effect on Your Life

Chapter 1

Getting Started

There is really no way to get around this than through it.

For example, we all fight with feelings of inadequacy. Think about that one person that inspires you to be more, do more, and who you probably think can never get to a point where he doubts his capacities. Would you be surprised to know that there are days when that same person feels as though he cannot be able to do anything worthwhile?

As interesting and unbelievable as this sounds, it is true. We all have our days of ups and downs. We all have the days when we begin to feel as though we are not able to achieve much. On those days, the tendencies to give in to fear, uncertainty, anxiety, and generally stress out over everything are much. But as you must have figured out, the difference between such persons doing all they can to make the world a better place and inspire thousands while at it, and those who burrow under their duvets and twiddle their thumbs while doing nothing is not the absence of fear but what they do with the fear they have.

Have you ever stopped to think about it for one minute? Those feelings of fear that course through your body as you begin to make plans for the future, the uncertainty, and the thin margin of doubt that makes you feel as though you are going to make a colossal mistake and crash into something terrible. Have you thought about what they mean and the effects those feelings have on your body system?

When pulling out of your shell to do something new and challenge your limits, tendencies are that you will have all these feelings course through your body. It is not strange to feel uncertainty in the face of these novel situations. In this chapter, we will look a bit into why your body has all those reactions whenever you are faced with anything that poses as some kind of challenge and will force you to step out of your cocoon of comfort.

How Our Brain Works When We Overthink

It would be counter-productive if we take you into the heart of overthinking, trying to help you out with it, and not taking time out to understand what happens whenever you begin to overthink things. That is why this section of this book was written - to take you behind the scenes and give you a clearer understanding of what happens in your brain whenever you begin stressing out over everything.

The first thing that is worthy of note in this context is that overthinking things is not just a nuisance in terms of the fact that it can keep you from being productive. Excessive overthinking can take a serious toll on your health and make you begin to experience some kind of deterioration in your body. When you begin to stress out about something, a few things start happening to you.

First off, you begin to experience anxiety. In the short run, anxiety can come in handy because the anxiety stimulus triggers a set of hormones in your brain, which are known as the flight-or-fight hormones. These hormones are responsible for the rush of energy you feel when you are anxious about something, and if channeled properly, it can be a good thing. However, when released in excess for an extended period of time, the anxiety can become dangerous because these hormones can zero in on your central nervous system, causing a long-term adverse effect. When anxiety is prolonged, these hormones begin to work on the central nervous system, and this results in feelings of nausea and light-headedness. As the moments begin to pass by, the feelings become worse and more intense. You begin to battle migraines, loss of concentration, and distorted thinking, and a lot of other terrible symptoms begin to manifest. If this is not curbed immediately, the mind can also begin to work simultaneously, and the job of the mind at this point will most likely be to make the situation appear worse than it is.

So, when you begin to overthink a decision you have made and the possible effects it can have, you begin to battle with anxiety. As a result of this, the anxiety begins to rise, and the physical symptoms increase with it. It keeps rising until it gets to a point where the symptoms peak and you may fall into a state of a panic attack.

In a nutshell, a lot of things happen when you begin to overthink things. The most striking of them all is the fact your brain functions begin to dwindle, you may begin to lose touch of your premium cognitive functions, and become prone to making bad decisions. If you do not keep it in check, having the habit of overthinking can have a bad toll on your health as the days unfold.

What Overthinking Is and Is Not

The chances are that you may have a few questions nagging at the back of your mind right now. One of the major questions that people ask when it comes to overthinking things, the anxiety that comes from it, and the discussion of why they should not let it happen to them, is the question of *should I then be careless?*

Having worked with countless people on this matter over time, and helping them bring the concept of overthinking things into perspective, it is vital that we lay emphasis on this subtopic. Having a clear understanding of what overthinking is and is not, will help us in the journey ahead of us.

1. Not overthinking things is not an excuse for carelessness. This is one of the points we must have to address so that we can form a healthy foundation for all we would be discussing in this book. In the previous sections of this book, we went into detail on how overthinking things can be a major deterrent that can stop you from reaching out into the future and taking charge of your tomorrow. We discussed how the best way to achieve things is by launching out into uncertainty and deciding to make the most out of it.

   However, this no way seeks to take the place of carefulness, planning, and meticulousness - especially as regards putting up strategies and processes that will get you to the goal you desire to get to.

   Many people see the advice - *stop overthinking it*

and launch out - as an excuse to begin projects they have not equipped themselves for. They have a warped understanding that *refusing to overthink it* means that they should give it no thought at all, but this is not the case. Not overthinking, it is simply what it is; refusing to give up on your plan of action because of the fear and uncertainty that lies in the execution of your tasks. It does not mean the refusal to put things in place, but it is the knowledge that even when things seem to be a bit bleak, there is always a way out, and that every task is executable.

2. Overthinking is entirely different from self-reflection. The difference sometimes is not in the activity being carried out, but in the intent that underlies and sponsors the activity being carried out. While self-reflection/analysis is carried out in a bid to critically examine aspects of a person's life with the intent to make changes and do better, overthinking is the same activity, but with the intent of spotting loopholes and challenges in a plan. Overthinking stops motion and positive

movement, while self-reflection is a massive tool that can be deployed in order to make progress and make the most out of all your efforts.
3. Overthinking is a process that is entirely self-limiting and counter-productive. This is because it dwells and focuses on all the things you do not have any control over, wishing that those can be changed. This, has never been the recipe for any successful person's success. Successful people are known to be the ones who do not spend all their time wishing that they had control over the things they have no control over. Rather, they take inventory of all the factors that are within their control, and with them, they are able to make the most of their lives.
4. Overthinking is the polar opposite of creative thinking. While creative thinking is the process of looking at challenges from a perspective of knowing that they can be solved, overthinking is that nagging feeling that what has happened has happened.

Creative thinking seeks to brainstorm ideas and

come up with solutions to any problem, but overthinking is geared toward journeying in circles and the inability to come up with solutions to problems that occur in real-time.

As we have seen in the points discussed above, overthinking is a recipe for disaster. This is because it takes away all the resources that are needed to come up with solutions to challenges, leaves the person drained (physically and emotionally), while still making sure that the person who overthinks remains at a spot for a very long time.

Causes of Overthinking

Since we have discussed a few things that pertain to overthinking, this question still holds to reason. Why do people still find themselves overthinking everything? Given the constraints and the results that we have listed out which happen as a result of overthinking, why is it that this is still a habit that is wide-spread?

These questions have given rise to what we will be discussing in this section of the book.

1. The major causes of overthinking lie in two words; *worry* and *anxiety*.

    If you take out time to take a look at all we have discussed so far, you will discover that these are the two major causes of overthinking. People tend to freak out and fixate on matters unhealthily when they are;

a. Worried about the outcome of something. Let us use this as a litmus test for you. The last time you spent time overthinking things on any matter, you will discover that the reason for that is because you were worried about something. Just as we have explained in the preceding sections of this book, worry causes a person to halt in their movement, start imagining a million different ways through which something can go bad, or spend quality time worrying about something that has happened in the past.

b. Anxious over matters that are still to arise or issues they have no control over. This is one of the major causes of overthinking, and when a person spends time in this mental and emotional

space, there is every tendency that the person may not get a lot of things done.
2. Another major cause of overthinking is the fact that we are usually bothered by what other people will think whenever we want to embark on new ideas or projects. When a person is about to get started on any project or do something that he has not done before, chances are that the people around him may be a bit averse to the new idea. As a result of this, he/she may end up halting shortly before executing the task. Once a person begins to pay less attention to the negative things he/she thinks people will say of any idea or project embarked on, he/she has greatly reduced the tendency to overthink things.
3. A pursuit for perfection: The thoughts which come up at the back of your mind every time you are about to embark on a major task and cause you to halt, can be traced directly to a pursuit of perfection. Statistics have shown that perfectionists (people who hold off on doing things because they want everything to be perfect

before they can get started with their projects) hardly ever get anything worthwhile done. The reason for this is because perfection hardly exists, and notwithstanding how good a thing is, there is always room for it to become better. Understand this, you may never be able to take a step in the right direction if you do not let go of the inordinate pursuit for perfection.

4. Another major cause of overthinking is a lack of confidence and the nagging fear that you did not do a great job with preparing for an assignment. Confidence on all fronts is usually sponsored by the knowledge that you are well-prepared for the execution of a task, and at any point, you discover that you lack the confidence required to get something done, there is every tendency that you will overthink it.

5. A self-centered perception of the world. The first thing we must establish here is this knowledge; not everything is about you. If you begin to see life and everything around you as being all about you, you may never take a step out of your

comfort zone. The reason for this is because you would not want to make a mistake and end up ruining the supposed image people have about you. In the process of not making a mistake, you will discover that you will never take any step to get anything worthwhile done.

Signs of Overthinking

If you are like Charles, you will notice that there are a few things that keep happening to you on a recurrent basis. These signs show up again and again, and they are suggestive of the fact that you are overthinking things. The aim of this section is to make you aware of these signs, and if you begin to notice these signs at the end of this section, then you need to take all that has and will be discussed in this book more seriously.

1. You find out that you are always caught in the vicious cycle of "wishing what could have been." People who overthink hardly ever make good use of what they have control over. They rather spend so much of their time and energy worrying over the things they do not have control over.

2. People who overthink cannot stop worrying and thinking along the lines of the negative "what ifs." What if it does not work out? What if I make a mess of myself? What if I don't get to achieve my goals. The only challenge is that they spend so much time and energy having bad thoughts of the millions of ways through which everything can possibly go south, and never seem to think on optimistic thoughts.
3. People who overthink never truly move on after making mistakes. They are not able to forgive themselves, learn the lessons from their mistakes, and move on with their lives. Rather, they spend time rehashing all that has happened to them, and as a result of this, they begin to lose out on their self-confidence. They have this nagging fear that they would repeat whatever they did before, and this time, in a worse way.
4. People who overthink have issues with their self-esteem. They do not believe that they can become or amount to anything good, and this is usually as a result of what has been discussed just above.

5. Another sign of overthinking is that people who overthink have an unhealthy fixation on the past. They recall conversations they have had and think of the things they should or should not have said, always remembering the things they should or should not have done in the past, and generally cannot seem to resign themselves to the fact that the past is where it is for a reason.
6. They are always on the lookout for what people have to say about them and the projects they start out. Before they get started doing anything worthwhile, they take their time gathering all the information they can, and at the shred of the slightest resistance, they give up on their goals and aspirations.

Effects of Overthinking

Throughout this book so far, we have talked about the effects overthinking things have on people. In this section of the book, we would quickly run through them for the sake of emphasis.

1. Overthinking stops you from being as productive

as you can be, and limits the boundaries of your creativity /innovation.
2. Overthinking can lead to a reduced sense of self-esteem. When all a person can think of are the mistakes he has made or all the ways he can make mistakes, these can result in him losing a grip on his self-esteem.
3. Overthinking can result in mental illnesses and physical health complications. Acute depression, panic attacks, consciously inflicting pain on oneself, amongst others, are a few of the results of overthinking things. Another major side effect of overthinking is insomnia. People who overthink things have been shown to hardly get enough rest at night or whenever they shut their eyes to sleep. This is because their brains can hardly be quiet long enough for them to sleep. This, in turn, has a direct effect on the quality of work they are able to produce the next day.
4. Overthinking is counter-productive. As we have said in the earlier sections of this chapter, overthinking steps in the way of the brain's

analytical and problem-solving skills. The result of this is that you spend so much time and resources worrying over the things you have lost or the things that could have been at the expense of your brain's ability to solve problems. When the brain is subjected to the tension and pressure that comes from overthinking, you will end up losing touch with your ability to solve problems.

<u>Summary</u>

Notwithstanding how you may want to take a look at it, overthinking is not a good thing for your body system and your ability to be productive. It stems from a lot of reasons, including the fear of what people will say, lack of confidence, and worry.

To be able to step out of this, you must first understand what overthinking is not. This is to enable you monitor yourself and know when you have begun to get into overthinking. There is no easy way to say it; overthinking is a habit that is counter-productive, and you must make it a point of duty to get it out of your life. This is the first step to a marked progress.

Chapter 2

Anxiety, Negative Thoughts, and Worry

What Triggers These Thoughts?

At some point in your life, you must have had these thoughts crawling through your mind. It does not matter how hard you try, there is every likelihood that you will experience these feelings often as you move through your everyday life.

We have talked about the signs that usually accompany anxiety and worry and in this section of the book, we will be discussing what triggers them. When you know exactly what triggers these, you will know how to avoid the triggers, what you must do to remain on top of these feelings and still be productive every time.

As you must have been able to deduce by now, anxiety, worry and these crippling fears are mental and psychological issues. Inasmuch as they are psychological, they have real physical effects and can result in symptoms that manifest in the body and can be seen with the naked eyes. According to the dictionary, anxiety is a state of mental uneasiness, nervousness, apprehension and obsession over an uncertain event. Thoughts of fear and anxiety can be triggered by a lot of physical and emotional factors, which include those we would be discussing shortly.

1. **Conflict;** Have you ever been in a brawl with someone over an issue before this time? Can you remember how it suddenly felt as though your heart was about to jump out of your chest and you could feel your temperature slowly rising? This is because one of the major triggers for anxiety and fear is conflict. This happens whenever there are arguments, disagreements between people, and even internal conflict can also trigger this. Whenever you are torn between doing something or not doing it, you will see that it is almost impossible for you to feel entirely relaxed until you have reached a final decision and executed on the task. This is one of the reasons why it is not good to entertain certain

thoughts and emotions within you. The buildup of emotions that come as a result of these emotions can trigger anxiety and worry within your system.

2. **Stress;** Another major trigger for the feelings of anxiety and worry is stress. Everyone gets to be stressed on an almost-daily level. Every day comes with its own stress factors, which range from major things like missing out on a looming deadline at work to other things like being stuck in traffic. However, when stress becomes long-term and happens constantly, it can lead to something more serious like long-term anxiety and other health conditions as well. However, when you are about to embark on a new project or step out of your shell to get on with something you have never done before, you most likely would begin to feel this stress. This is a normal phenomenon, and all you can do is to manage the feelings of stress that will come. How you will be able to achieve that is discussed in-depth in the subsequent chapters of this book.

3. **Health challenges;** There are some new health issues that can be quite jarring. Imagine the look on the face of a man that has just come to know that he has a terminal disease such as cancer or a tumor that is life-threatening. That piece of information opens up the door and the person instantly begins to feel the effects of anxiety and worry as these feelings begin to build up in his body system. Health challenges are a major trigger for anxiety. Also related to this is the use of medication.

   Due to their constituents and the nature of their operation, there are some medications that have the side effects of creating in people the feelings of anxiety and stress. Drugs like birth control pills, congestion medication and medication given for strong health challenges are known to be triggers of anxiety. The nature of what they do in the body system gives rise to these feelings of anxiety they trigger in the body.

4. **Phobias;** These are relatively common with people today. There is every possibility that you

may have met someone with some form of phobia in your life. This could be the phobia for heights (vertigo), claustrophobia (fear of little spaces), and every other kind of fear. These fears are usually crippling and come with feelings of intense worry and anxiety.

5. **The threat of harm and the fear of the unknown;** This happens to be one of the most widely-known causes of worry and anxiety today. The harm being spoken of in this context can either be real or imagined. As we discussed in the earlier parts of this book, you would most likely feel anxious and fearful when you are about to venture into things you have not done before. Also, there are many thoughts that cross your mind on a daily basis that if you do not play an active part to nip them in the bud, they can become a very serious instrument to keep you worried and anxious for the rest of your life. These are the *what-ifs*. "What if I don't come back today because I have been crushed by a car?" "What if this project fails and I lose all my money?" "What if my boss fires me

and I do not know what else to do?" the list of what-ifs is endless.

There is always that margin of uncertainty in life. This is because there are things that are within your control and others that are not within your control. If you spend the whole day fixating on the *what-ifs* and those things that you have no control over, you will discover that you will be kept from reaching the zenith of your powers and you will be incapacitated to a very large extent. Letting go of these fears is a key part of your success, and that is what we will be fully looking into in the later chapters of this book.

6. **Fear and anxiety;** can also be triggered by physical stimuli like the sudden loss of visibility, darkness, the sudden appearance of a harmful object, or a wild animal. This aspect of fear is one that many people have to deal with on a daily basis.

7. Another major trigger for negative thoughts are **words and what other people say to you**. If you

interact with people who are confident of your abilities and do not keep their convictions to themselves but let you know that they believe in you, you will discover that you will have a level of confidence and emotional boost that comes as a result of the words they say. On the other hand, if the people around you are cynical, do not think you can achieve much, and do not hesitate to let you know what they think about you, you will discover that there are chances that you will end up battling worry at every point.

As a pro-tip here, if you want to be above worry and learn how to do the things you need to do irrespective of the fear of the unknown and worry, you need to spend a good amount of time scrutinizing what you hear and what the people around you say to you.

8. **Over-analysis and unhealthy rumination;** will most likely lead to negative thoughts. While it is vital that you spend a reasonable amount of time planning out your life and analyzing the success of the ventures you are about to get into, if not

moderated, you may end up entertaining negative thoughts. This is because the more you analyze the steps you are about to take, the more the chances of accessing the alternatives more than the step you want to take. So, instead of thinking about the success of the venture you are about to get into, you may end up dreaming up a million ways things can get bad very quickly.

The result of this is that after a season of not being able to execute on your plans, you will discover that you will begin to have negative thoughts of yourself. This will begin to affect your productivity and sense of self-esteem. Low self-esteem usually comes with self-deprecation and negative thoughts of self.

Anxiety, worry and negative thoughts have a lot more triggers than have been discussed in this section. The aim of this section was to get you to see that a lot of triggers exist for these things and that you must make it a point of duty to spot them out and keep yourself from coming in contact with them often. It is not enough to know what triggers anxiety, worry and negative thoughts; what matters more than knowing this is what you do after you have spotted these triggers.

In subsequent parts of this book, we will be taking a look at proven strategies to get you started on the right track to managing these emotions and still being as productive as you can possibly be.

Write Them Down in a Journal

If you are someone who has seen the value of writing and how it can be of immense benefit to you, then you would know that there is more to writing than just putting pen to paper. Many people have learned the value of writing down their goals, aspirations and dreams, but they have not been taught that writing down their fears is a great way to getting them obliterated. One of the proven strategies of dealing with fear and anxiety is the process of writing them down on paper.

When followed back to the beginning, you will discover that there are many people who began writing simply because of the therapeutic effects of putting pen to paper. When faced with the challenges they had to grapple with and threatened by the imminent fear of hitting rock bottom, they followed the path of journaling and this marked the beginning of a new era for them.

When faced with fears that seem to be recurrent, and battling the anxiety that comes with these fears, it has been discovered that one of the ways to make sure that you are not sucked under the currents of fear is to let out some of the steam. You can achieve this by active journaling.

Now that you know the triggers of fear, anxiety and worry, and you have taken it a step further by discovering exactly what triggers your anxiety, the next step you need to take is the step of listing out all these triggers you have identified. When you do this, you will discover that you have completed a major part of the tasks that will lead you to overcome those fears and move on to the life you want to live. Effective journaling is a great way to face your fears, but the real question is why.

Why You Should Write Them Down

The question that is going through your mind now is why. Why should you take out the time to begin to make a list of all the things you are afraid of and the triggers you have identified for fear and worry?

There are a few reasons for that, and we will be discussing a few of them.

1. The first reason why you need to write down your fears is that you need to get them out of the back of your mind. Here is the thing about fear; once fear is lodged in the deep parts of your mind, it appears to be a lot bigger than it actually is. This is a proven act, and that is why scientists and experts advise that you take out time to itemize your fears.

   When you do this, you are exposing those fears to the light of day. Like everything else, when you expose them to the light of day, you begin to see just how big they really are. Writing down your fears affords you the luxury of exercising the power you really have over them.

2. Putting your fears down on paper gives your brain the luxury of space needed to think. Now that you are beginning to declutter your mind of the fears that have been in them, you will see that it becomes easier for you to begin to think creatively. When you put down your fees and the causes of your anxiety on paper, it is easier for you to begin to brainstorm ideas that will lead you to the point you want to get to, the place of finding a lasting solution.

    This is possible because of the principle of mind mapping, which allows you to take a look at objectives, goals and fears from different points of view. Once you have started looking at your fears from different points of view, you would be more exposed to different options and ways to tackle them.

3. One sure way of processing anxiety is by writing about it. A major reason why you feel too much when you are anxious is because of the fact that there is too much haziness to your feelings. You have an idea of what is going on within you at

the moment, but you are not able to tell exactly what it is you are feeling. When you begin to put words to your anxiety and write them down on paper, you are able to articulate EXACTLY how you feel. The result of this is that you end up with a clear picture of what your worry is like, what is the cause of the anxiety, and as a result, it is easier for you to tackle the problems at hand.

4. Writing down your fears is a therapeutic way of getting them off your chest. Consider your journal to be the ears of a compassionate health specialist who wants to be of help to you. When you write them down, you are able to get some of the weight off your chest and although the journal may not proffer solutions, it provides a great tool for you to be able to get started with the process of figuring things out.

5. Writing down your fear and anxiety triggers give you a clear idea of what to avoid and what to steer clear of. When you have the knowledge of the things that get you stressed, and you know the effects of getting worried and anxious every

time, you will do your best o make sure that you do not always fall into the trap of those triggers. This is a great way to keep your hands on the reins of your sanity.

Now that you have seen the value in writing down your fears and anxiety, here is an idea on how to start keeping an effective anxiety journal.

1. Come to terms with the kind of personality you have. There are people who tend to be more stressed than others. These people get easily riled up and anxious over things. If you are this kind of person, you may need this more than others who are less likely to get worried over everything. When you have done this, you will see the need for sticking this through until the end.
2. Have a clear goal for journaling. Understand that the goal is not for you to magnify your fears and anxiety over what they truly are, bout to get them out of the back of your mind and into the light of day so that you can begin to address them properly. This knowledge will guide you as you

begin to write.

3. Be entirely honest with yourself as you put pen to paper. This journal is your sacred property and no one is allowed to have access to it. As a result of this, you are allowed to be very open and talk about how you feel. The first step to obliterating fear, anxiety and worry using this strategy is by ensuring that you are honest with yourself. Not being entirely honest is like hitting the hammer everywhere else but on the head of the nail. You will only end up journeying in circles.

4. Start making lists. This is a list of what to make lists of;

a. Make a list of your fears and the things that cause you to get anxious.

b. Think back and make a list of the sources of those fears. Where did they come from? At what point did you pick them up? This knowledge will help you know exactly what you are dealing with.

c. At the back of that fear is something very valuable to you. Find out what that thing is and write it down. For example, the fear of starting out a business only exists because of the possibility of that business idea blooming and becoming the next best thing. If it was not a business idea, you wouldn't have harbored thoughts of it in the first place.

d. Channel your attention to the value you have now identified, instead of the fear. In doing this, make a list of how you can be able to make that value you have identified to be manifested towards you. For example, instead of stressing out about how the business will fail, focus on other ideas like studying the business model very well, getting mentors to guide you and wise business partners. This way, you will end up knowing what you should focus your energy on.

5. Now that you have a list of the things you need to focus on, make a commitment to focus on them. With this commitment should go the desire to get

started. When you have gotten to this point, *ruthless execution* becomes the code. You do not overcome fear by being afraid of fear, you overcome fear be moving on despite the fear.

<u>Summary</u>

Anxiety, worry and thoughts of fear have a strong way of taking away from your productivity and keeping you in a spot for a very long time. If you are going to break out and achieve all you want to achieve, you must be willing to shed these feelings and go for the things you really want to achieve.

Section II

Strategies To Stop Overthinking

Chapter 3

Ending Negativity and Embracing Positivity

Reflect on the Bright Side of Life Everyday

This is easier said than done. In the world we live today, it is easy to make a decision to reflect on the bright side of life and make a decision to show optimism in everything you do, but it is actually difficult to carry this singular act out.

This may be owing to a lot of reasons ranging from the fact that there is every tendency that you will come to hear of something negative once you put on the television to see the news in the morning, to the fact that your neighbor could annoy you to the point that you may feel like doing something irrational. The unpredictable state of today's world makes it very difficult for a man to just make a decision to be optimistic and keep a happy approach to life and actually get to stick to this decision.

Seeing as it is vital to do this, here are a few reasons why you must make a commitment to always reflect on the bright side of life every single day.

1. The most obvious thing that looking on the bright side of life and the experiences you have will do to you is that it will make you develop a positive mental disposition towards the world. This is known as a positive mindset and is very vital to success. Science and research carried out over the years have revealed that to be successful, you must make it a point of duty to work on your mindset to such an extent that you develop a mindset that is positive and looks at the world from the standpoint of a winner. This is one of the things that looking at things from the bright perspective will do to you.

   So instead of bemoaning the fact that you got a query from your boss in the workplace, you can make it a point of duty to take a look at things from the bright side. Doing this will make you rephrase the whole experience to be something like your boss just called you to remind you that tardiness is not a trait that successful employees have. You can also take the opportunity to make a commitment that he will only see a better version of you moving forward. That is one way to take a look at it, and if done this way, you will see that you would have created more space for you to grow in your career and to become more effective.

2. Looking at the positive side of things leaves little or no room for stress. With the surge of energy that comes from that mindset shift, you will discover that you will be imbued with an energy that would not have been there if all you did was stare at the wall all day and feel sorry for the things that have happened to you. As discussed earlier, worry and stress can arise from a lot of reasons, including the fear that you do not have what it takes to control a situation. However, when you begin to look at the bright side of

things, you will notice that you will begin to see yourself from the light of a person that has power over the situation. As a result, you will discover that you will begin to lose the stress that comes with it and in place of that, a sense of control begins to rise up from within you.

3. A research carried out by a team of doctors and scientists revealed that having a positive outlook toward life will help you survive health challenges of many types. As much as it is difficult to maintain a positive outlook towards life when you must have been informed of an impending health challenge, a decision to live from the place of looking at the positive side of life and having an optimistic approach to it will make your chances of being healthy for a very long time to increase the more.

As opposed to those who sit and wallow in pity, you will have more chances to be more productive and achieve more if you can take a look at things from the bright side of life.

Now that we have made a list of the benefits you stand to gain by looking at the bright side of life, here are a few practical steps you can apply to make sure that you are able to get this done.

1. Do a mental sweep of the people in your life, and commit to cleaning up the fodder. There are people in your life who have nothing to give but toxicity. These are people who come to you with nothing but bad news. They do not call you when something good happens, like getting married or getting a promotion. They only call and come close when they have a piece of bad information to share. These guys are not supposed to be in your life, because they will make all your efforts go south in a matter of minutes. In the same vein, make a mental sweep of the people in your life and begin to spot out those ones who have made it a point of duty not to see your value, and who

do not believe in the life you are called to live. In place of having those people in your life (alongside the bad energy they bring with them), make a commitment to cut them out. They are nothing but fodder to your life and where you are headed, and you honestly do not need the encumbrance they will bring to your table.
Guard your space jealously.

2. Look inwards. This is also one of the first things you must do if you are going to be able to start out with being positive always. It is not enough to start cutting people who are not contributing to your success out of your life. If you do not make a commitment to work on your own self, be rest assured that nothing will happen for you. Look within you and make a strong commitment that notwithstanding what happens around you, you will never get to a point where you feel so down and uninspired. It begins with yourself and the burning desire to get more done with your life.

3. Practice gratitude, and make it a daily habit. This is one of the secrets of highly successful people; they have made practicing gratitude a part of their daily habits. This is a very simple task, and it entails that you notice every last good thing that happens to you every day. When you are done noticing the little details and the God things that have happened to you that day, write them down in a journal. This practice may be hard to keep up at first, but the aim is to get you to a place where you develop the eye that has been trained to see the good things and a reason to be grateful in every situation.

4. Whenever you are about to be overwhelmed by negative thoughts and the reality of the fact that life can be bad, commit to fixating on thinking good thoughts. There has to be a silver lining to hold on to in the midst of every storm, right? That is the same thing you do once you carry out this exercise. For every time you are about to be overwhelmed by something negative, pick out a

memory from your past and fixate on it. Let it be a memory that puts a smile on your face. Doing this will make sure that you are not overwhelmed by the feelings of weakness that come with thinking of negativity all the time.

5. Talk to someone. Sometimes, it may not be easy for you to achieve this all by yourself, and that is why it becomes vital for you to talk to someone. It may be a therapist or a trusted person who can help you out of the dark place, but the goal is to make sure that you do not sink into the pool of feeling bad when you can reach out to someone who can offer some sort of help to you.

Live in the Present

We pointed out earlier that one major reason why people never seem to be able to live to the peak of their abilities is that they spend way too much time fussing over the past (which they cannot change) or stressing out about the future (which is yet to happen). The result of this is that they hardly ever get to live in the present, and if you do not live in the present, then you do not have any hopes of achieving anything remarkable.

Goal-oriented people know that if they must achieve the things that they have set out to achieve, they owe it to themselves and to the people around them to live in the moment. They know this because they have been in the place where they stressed out about everything that was not the present, and they were able to tell after a long time that all they did was just waste their time. Here are a few reasons why you must live in the present.

1. Have this knowledge and be very clear about it; the past is in the past for a reason. There is nothing you can do to change it, and the only positive way to take a look at your past is to try and draw lessons from it that you can apply to the present in order to change the future.

   For example, a man who has just been relieved of his job can make a choice to live in the days when he had his past job. He can choose to sit down all day and bemoan the fact that he was sacked, or he can decide to take a look at his contribution to the whole thing. It could have been that he was not as productive as he should have been, or that there were other reasons why he was relieved. In place of crying incessantly about the job he lost, he can take it upon himself to improve his skill set so that he can become an employable worker in another firm, and be more productive at his new job. This is the mindset you must adopt if you are going to start living in the present.

2. There are times it helps for you to get off your mind from the big goal and focus on the small wins that will get you to your big goal. Let's face it; it is a great thing to feel that rush of dopamine and feel elated at the thoughts that you have a big goal to meet. However, it can be daunting to just keep an eye on the goal. So instead of looking at the big goal and getting discouraged at how insurmountable it seems, focus more on the little wins that will culminate in the big goal. Instead

of stressing out about how far your Ph.D. seems to be from you, focus on acing all your courses in all your exams and you would be surprised at how fast you will end up getting to the big goal you have set for yourself.

3. Understand that even the best of plans is not that foolproof. One of the reasons why you never get much done (as we have discussed earlier) is the fact that you spend a lot of time planning and analyzing how you will have the perfect thing happen for you. While it is great to be meticulous, it is worthy to note that even the best and most detailed plans are still not immune to suffering from a few unforeseen circumstances. This knowledge will make you know that the best thing to do is to live in the now and take the days as they show up. Things do not always happen as you would want them to, and it is best you have this in mind as you walk through your everyday life.

Here are a few steps to helping you live in the present.

1. Make your long-term goals, but focus on the short-term wins that will get you there. Instead of looking at the enormity of the goals and fixating on how impossible it may seem, break it down into actionable steps and focus more on the little steps. All those steps put together will result in the actualization of the goals you have set for yourself.

2. Understand that every moment is a gift and that the next is not guaranteed. This way, you do not spend the gift you have received doing something that is not worthwhile.

3. While it is good to let go of the past, never let go of the lessons you learned from the past. They will come in handy to save you time in the present and guide the decisions you will be making in the future. Pick up the lessons from the

past and treasure them as though they were very important to you because they actually are.

Change the Way You Think: Gratitude Vs. Regret

Regrets have never been famed to be helpful in any way. They only take away from the present the energy that you should use in making things work for yourself. In place of regrets and the knowledge that comes from the fact that you could have done something better in the past, it is best that you approach this subject matter from the point of gratitude.
Here are a few quick things you can do to take you from the place of regrets to the place of gratitude.

1. See the past for what it truly is. No one regrets things that have not yet happened to them. Instead of isolating the things that have gone down in your life, feeling ashamed of them, and doing nothing to change them, take a look at your past and compartmentalize the things that have happened in it where they should be. There is

nothing you can do to change the past, you can only take lessons from it and move on.

2. Look out for the blessing in everything. This would be difficult for you, especially if you are starting out with it for the first time, but it is very vital that you do not skip this step. In every pain you have experienced, there is a blessing. The blessing could be a lesson that you have learned. Take this blessing and make a point of duty to be grateful for it. One way to get this to be a part of your life is by making a gratitude journal. This is a book where you write down all the things that have happened to you, and the good things you have come to learn and experience as a result of them. Make a habit of writing this every day, and you will be surprised at the mind shift you will experience.

Act with Confidence

Confidence is a major part of successful people. If you are going to be able to achieve anything remarkable, and influence others into achieving the same results for themselves, you must be able to begin by working on your confidence level and becoming the person you want to be seen as.

Many times, people who lace confidence chuck the whole thing up to being shy. They have the tendency to isolate everything that happens to them and deciding that these things happen because they are shy people. When looked at from this perspective, it becomes dangerous because you begin to leave a lot to fate, and undermine the fact that you have a role to play towards becoming better.

If you have found out that you are not as confident as you would love to be, there are a few handy hacks that can help you gain your desired confidence level. Here are a few of them.

1. Start by mastering something useful in today's world. Most of the feelings of lack of confidence, and the tendency to hide from it is as a result of

the knowledge that you are not too good in an area. For example, if you were a very skilled writer, you would not shy away from taking up tasks that relate to writing when the opportunity comes up. If, on the other hand, you were a terrible writer, you would pass over any opportunity to do anything that relates to putting pen to paper. This is the same way it happens in your life. It could be your skill, passion, or the career path you have chosen; the goal is to make sure that you are so good in one thing. This is the first step to actually becoming confident of yourself and the things you can do.

2. Stop having all those negative self-talk and limiting notes-to-self. One of the major reasons you may be battling with your confidence level may be because you are still making it a habit to have all those conversations that remind you of how incapacitated you are in many areas of your life. If you still allow that little voice that pops out of your head to still tell you that you are not good

enough, then that is exactly what is going to happen to you; you will remain small and unable to achieve anything. In place of all these conversations with yourself that do not produce much good, how about you start out with making positive affirmations that boost your confidence every day until you learn to start believing them?

3. Look the part. If you want to act and appear confident at all times, then it is up to you to make it a point of duty to look the part at all times. Fix your posture; get rid of that slouched posture and droop in your shoulders, square up, chest out and walk with your head high. While you are at it, remember to dress as though you are a confident person. This is one way to make sure that you are perceived as confident, and that you actually start increasing your confidence levels. People first see you before anything else, hence the need to fix your physical appearance.

4. Surround yourself with people that see your value, understand your worth, and do not

hesitate to communicate this to you. If you want to become confident, find yourself in the company of the confident ones, and you will be surprised at what will happen to you. Notwithstanding how good you are in a thing, there will be days when you would need to be reassured by some people that you can. That is why it is good for you to have them around you already.

Summary

While moving on to become more productive and stop battling with the things that keep you from achieving all you want to achieve, there are a few hints you must take care of. These things seem little, but compared to the effects they have in the big picture and the results of their accumulation, you may be surprised to discover how big they really are. That is why you need to adopt the little cues that have been discussed in this chapter and keep them all in mind.

Chapter 4

Create a To-Do List

Productive people and those who have put a lot of their energies toward making the most out of their lives can all agree that there is one thing that is known to bring order and a sense of being in control of a person's life.

Let us be honest for a while; you are probably pressed for time. You may be the kind of person who has to be up in the morning and throughout the day and struggling to keep up with the activities you have to ensure you execute. You are known for trying to juggle a lot every time because every last day shows up with its own share of challenges and the pressure to pull you in all directions. You retire every night with the nagging feeling that you did not complete all that you were supposed to complete for the day, and as a result, you spend the next day trying to do what you were supposed to do the previous day.

The result of this is that you never get to have a fully productive day, and you may have even come to conclude that you may just start needing twenty-five hours in your own day. Well, here's the thing about time, and the tasks you have to accomplish per day.

You will have to understand that you may never have enough time to do all the things that you want to do every day. Each day comes with a myriad of tasks to accomplish, goals to meet, things to do, and all the rest. The result is that it is hardly ever possible to get all these done on a regular basis. As a result of this reality, many people have come to believe that making effective use of to-do lists is a great lifesaver. In this chapter of the book, we will be taking a quick look at the concept of to-do lists and the proper way of making sure that you use them to get the most you can get.

How Your Life would be Without a To-Do List

Imagine trying so hard to step away from quicksand without external help. So, let us say you decided to take a walk into the forest near your country house, to just enjoy nature for a cool evening. In your journey through the wild, you make the mistake of stepping into quicksand, which you never know was there. The worst part is that there is no one within sight to help pull you out of the sand you are quickly sinking into.

It is a very bad thought, and as much as you do not want to think that something like that can happen to you, that is exactly what happens every time you try to live your life without a to-do list.

The activities of every day are like quicksand; overwhelming, have what it takes to suck all the energy out of you, and the worst is that the more you try to wriggle free from them, the more you see that you are being sucked under the weight of the workload of each day. Making it a habit to face each day without a clear outline of the tasks you have to accomplish for the day will result in the following;

1. A sense of being unfulfilled. If you are not able to complete all that you should every day, you will retire at night with those feelings that you could have accomplished more. This may not be the best because those feelings can drain you of all your strength and leave you trying to accomplish

the next day, what you should have done the previous day.

2. Disorganization comes from not having a laid down path you would love to follow every day. Since the to-do list comes with an outline of the tasks you want to accomplish every day, and in the order that you would love to get that done, it takes away a lot of disorganization and unnecessary spontaneity.

3. Without a to-do list, there is every tendency that your productivity levels will tank. This is because you will be unable to focus on tasks at hand, and commit to finishing them one at a time. Instead, you will end up trying to multi-task, and the result is that you will end up achieving nothing of value under those circumstances.

Many things will go wrong with your day if you do not make it a practice of making use of to-do lists and sticking it through. The bottom line of all of these things that will happen is that your productivity will be greatly tampered with. If you are looking to increase productivity, then take the practice of creating daily to-do lists as seriously as you can.

How a To-Do List Helps with Overthinking

A to-do list helps you stop overthinking things, and increases your productivity by;

1. Ensuring you focus on the now. As we have pointed out earlier, one of the major reasons why you are not too productive is because you are either stuck in the past or fixating on the future in a bad way. You are never in the present, and that is when the moments slip away from your grasp. To ensure that this will stop happening, you may want to incorporate to-do lists into your everyday routine.

2. Having a to-do list ensures that you do not forget to do anything. It helps you with your meticulousness, and this will, in turn, increase

your productivity levels. You tend to overthink and worry about the things you could have done whenever you end your day not achieving all you should have. Having a well-arranged to-do list will help you avoid this.

3. When you have created a to-do list, you will have a clear understanding of the tasks that are worth your attention and those that are not. When you have decided what tasks are vital to the actualization of your goals, you can focus on them and channel all you have towards their achievement. This is one way to increase your productivity and stop overthinking/stressing out about the things you should probably not be worried about in the first place.

Maintain a To-Do List & Stick to it

It is not enough to create a to-do list. Much more than that is the commitment to stick to it. Doing this (creating a to-do list) is just like making every decision you make in your life on a daily basis. If you do not back up the decision making with the required action, you will be shocked to discover that decision making is not enough – at all.

This is one of the reasons why many people keep on making to-do lists every day, and they do not see any increase in their productivity levels. They just put things down on paper, and never make the commitments to follow through till they have accomplished what they wrote down, in the order they wrote it down.

When you have created a to-do list, the next thing you want to do is to set up structures that will help you stick to it. It is not easy to refrain from giving in to the ever-increasing temptation of letting go at every point during the day and moving with the tide which the day tosses your way.

Here are a few things that will help you commit to making use of your to-do list, and seeing it through till the end.

1. Commit to making use of only one to-do list app. While this may look tough, it is a great way to reinforce the fact that you are a goal-oriented person. When you use multiple to-do list apps, there is the tendency that in a bid to become more productive and start getting more things done every day, you slip into the trap of not making the most out of your time and efforts. The more productivity apps you have, the more the tendencies that you will set up different tasks on these applications. When different tasks are set up, it leads to a clash of interests and each of these tasks will be vying for your attention. The end of all these is that you are overwhelmed, and you won't be able to make the most out of your to-do lists efforts.

2. Be clear about the tasks on your lists. Ambiguity will always lead to confusion, and once your mind is not able to grasp something fully, there can be no commitment to complete it.

3. You may need to get an accountability partner. This is one of the most effective tricks that you can employ if you are going to be successful with any venture. You may need someone who can check up on you at the end of every day, just to make sure that you were able to complete the tasks that you set out to complete. If possible, let this person be a mentor or someone in a position over you. The knowledge that someone of that pedigree will soon call you to make inquiries will put upon you a sense of urgency, and you will soon see that you will begin to concentrate and commit to the things you start out.

4. Practice the use of rewards. As you begin to create your to-do lists for each day, decide how you want to reward yourself at the end of the tasks. It could be that at the end of the week, you are going to do something that you love doing, or that when a particular goal is accomplished, you will do "this thing." Rewards have a way of incentivizing your brain and body to commit to

the process they have to go through in order to make sure that you meet the goals you have set out for yourself.

Creating an Effective To-Do List

Creating an effective to-do list is more work than just putting pen to paper and writing out all that you want to achieve in a day. There is a skill to doing this, and if you are able to understand the things that are involved in creating a to-do list that is minimalistic, effective and still comprehensive, then you have figured out a huge aspect of making proper use of to-do lists.

In order to create an effective to-do list, make use of the following steps;

1. Know that your to-do list does not have to include all the tasks in the world. There is only so much you can get done in one day, so have that at the back of your mind as you set out to create your to-do list.

2. Perform a brain dump. Although we have said that your to-do list does not have to incorporate a lot of things, it is not at this point that you begin to trim. Get a sheet of paper, or your mobile device and begin to make a list of the things you must do the next day. For this to be impactful, it is very wise that you make your to-do list every night before the morning. This is to enable your mind to have enough time to mull on the tasks for the next day and begin to devise strategies to get things done in a seamless way, even as you sleep through the night.

3. When you are done with making a list, begin to trim. At this point, it seems as though there is nothing that can go off the list but take some time to look at that list – critically. There are definitely things that can and should go out of that list. Spot them and begin to take them away. They could be tasks that are not too necessary that you can delegate, or that can wait for a much later date. Spot all of them, and take them off your list.

4. Now that you have a thinner list take the time to plan this list. Take a critical look at the individual tasks on the list and decide which comes first. Let the high-value tasks (those that have the most impact on your life, career and business) become first. In the same way, make a new list of these tasks and be sure to make this list in the order the tasks will come. First things first – bear that in mind as you make this new list.

5. Make your list minimal and do all you can to remove ambiguity. This means that you should remove as many tasks as can be removed from the list, and spell out all you have to do in clear terms. As much as it lies within you, use simple words in your list; you are not looking to impress anyone. This will help you focus better, and helps your mind capture a clearer image of what you have to achieve. Once this is done, you will begin to feel a rush of excitement at the prospects of getting it done.

6. Do the groundwork before time. If there is a task that requires you to make some preparations before the time to execute it comes, do that background work before time. For example, if one of your tasks is to reach out to prospective clients for your business, it will make more sense for you to compile a list of the people you want to reach out to before the time comes. This way, you do not spend the time that is needed to get the main task done in doing the preliminaries that will not have the same effect as when the main task is completed.

7. Create blocks of time to unwind and relax. Inasmuch as you have a lot to deal with, it is advisable that you do not choke up your to-do list with activities to such an extent that you do not get enough time to relax and unwind. Unwinding helps you to recharge your body, and your mind takes that much needed time to reboot. This way, you return to your task with more focus and increased precision.

8. Make space to tick off tasks and always check in with your accountability partner. There is nothing more satisfying than seeing that you are ticking off boxes in your to-do list. That knowledge brings a lot of joy and is a great propeller for you to keep going. As you complete tasks, do not forget to tick them off your list. Again, make it a point of duty to check in with your accountability partner and report progress at the end of every day or week.

<u>Summary</u>

It is very easy to slip into the pressure that comes with the overwhelming list of things you have to do each day. As much as there is every tendency for this list to keep increasing, you have a duty to ensure that you keep yourself within check, and stick to a plan of activities for each day.

Your to-do list does so much to you and your productivity than just giving you a roadmap to follow each day. It serves to give you focus and help you start living in the moment. This is an invaluable tool when it comes to your degree of productivity and the amount of work you can get done at the end of each day. Apply the principles and the tricks that have been shared in this chapter to make the most out of this venture.

Chapter 5

Live a Minimalistic Lifestyle

Minimalism is a practice that will undoubtedly change your life if you understand what it is and how to go about it. This is the honest truth; sometimes, your productivity is hampered because you are still yet to master how to take charge of your environment – both physically, emotionally, psychologically, and in all aspects. In this chapter, we will be discussing the cure to this inability to concentrate on tasks that result from the fact that you are still yet to master your surroundings.

The cure is encapsulated in one word – minimalism. If you are able to understand this and apply the practice to your life accordingly, you will see that after a season, your productivity game would have improved.

What is Minimalism?

Minimalism is a style or form of art that emphasizes extreme simplicity. In real life, minimalism is the practice of intentionally promoting the things we most value and the deliberate elimination of things that are not as valued, and which distract us from holding on to and making the most out of the things we most value.

The practice of minimalism hinges around the understanding of what truly matters in your life, and it results in a careful elimination of those that do not matter. When we talk about minimalism, it spans across every aspect of life, including the physical property you acquire and allow to remain in your space, the things you dedicate your time to doing, the people you allow to be in your circle, and every other thing in-between.

Minimalists (those practicing minimalism) agree that this lifestyle is one of the easiest ways to be very productive, love and at peace with yourself, and always be at your A-game at every single time of the day. This is because as much as you may not want to admit it, the things you allow to remain in your physical, emotional, mental and relational spaces will always affect the way you live and the way you react to the situations that come your way on a daily basis. A person who has fewer dishes in his house has fewer dishes to wash when it is time to do that assignment and hence has more time to concentrate on the things that are more important to him when the chips are down.

As you journey through getting comfortable with minimalism, remember that less is always more, but there are specific ways to go about getting this done.

Benefits of a Minimalist Lifestyle

Many people have refused to adopt the practice of minimalism, simply because they are yet to see the benefits that they stand to gain if they can subscribe to this way of living. In this section of the chapter, we will be talking about the benefits of minimalism.

1. The practice of minimalism helps you bring a lot of things into perspective and to help you decide

what is truly important to you. When you are in the process of taking away the clutter, and those things that do not make much sense being in your space, you will be forced to take a look at things from a more holistic point of view and you will make critical decisions as to what goes and what stays. You will most likely need all the dishes in your house, all the clothes in the closet, all the diaries on your work table, and all the tools in your shed until you decide that it is time to let some of them go. When you have made that decision, and you are committed to seeing it through until the end, you will be surprised at the things that will be leaving your space at the end of the day.

2. The practice of minimalism helps you with a sense of feeling centered and in control of your physical space. When you have started taking away the clutter, you will discover that there will be a sense of "being in control" that will start taking over you. It feels choking to be in a place

that is full of many things, and it can even appear as though all the things in your physical space are threatening to choke you away from there.

Whenever you begin to battle those feelings, just know that it is time to begin to take out the trash. When you begin to get things pout of the way, your sense of "being the one that is in charge" is reinforced, and your productivity levels begin to rise alongside it.

3. The practice of minimalism helps you to focus on the things that really matter to you. Just as you must have picked up by now, the aim of getting unnecessary things out from your space (physically, mentally, emotionally, and in all wise), is for the singular reason of getting you to focus on the things that really matter to you and that make the difference in the long run. When all the clutter is gone, you can go ahead to focus on the things that are vital to your well-being.

4. The practice of minimalism increases your happiness. This is the result of the culmination of all the little wins you will get as you begin to practice minimalism. When your productivity is increased, and you begin to feel in control of the space you are in, your focus spikes, and every other thing that has been discussed earlier happens to you, you will end up becoming a happier version of yourself.

5. Minimalism will help you boost your self-image and confidence. When you stop relying solely on the accumulation of physical properties, you will elevate the practice of looking inwards and drawing your emotional boost from within. This is one thing that will inadvertently lead to a healthier sense of self-esteem.

6. The practice of minimalism can go a long way to aid you on your journey to financial independence. When you focus more on getting and owning only the things that really matter to you, the temptation to make unwise financial

decisions like spontaneous shopping or the inordinate desire to accumulate things you won't be needing, in the long run, would diminish.

How to Live a Minimalistic Lifestyle

Inasmuch as we have buttressed the fact that less is more – as far as minimalism goes – it is also necessary that we establish a fact. The pursuit of minimalism does not mean that you should pack up all your belongings and fling them out the door. There is an approach to this, and if you will adopt a minimalist lifestyle and still feel the effects over a sustainable period of time, it is best you apply the strategies discussed in this section of the book.

1. Minimalism begins as a mindset. Even if you are to bundle up all that you have and give them out right now, if you are yet to have this mindset shift, you will see that in no time, all the things you have given out will return. The mindset of minimalism is one that adopts it as a vital principle, sees the need for it and adapts to the

fact that whatever it does not need should not be around it. This is the place to start your journey to minimalism from; the place of adjusting your mindset towards it.

2. Start the exercise by setting clear goals for yourself. It is necessary to note that in this matter, there is no one-size-fits-all approach. There is really no universal rule as to what you should have and the things that you should not have. The practice of minimalism gives you a code to live by and allows you to make the decisions by yourself. There would be no chaperone, so you would have to set CLEAR goals for yourself. What does minimalism look like to you? You may want to spell that out first, and attach a deadline to this task you are about to embark on.

3. Invest in materials that are top-quality and very durable. One of the reasons you may have more than three of any items may be because all three of them are not of the best quality there is. How

about you take time to invest in things that are of better quality and have more functionalities than others? Instead of having a printer, and a photocopier and a scanning machine pile up in your workplace, how about you invest in getting one of those multipurpose machines that have all three components in them?

4. Discipline yourself to live with less, refrain from spontaneous shopping, and actually stick to the process of living with only the things that really matter to you. Here's a warning, though; it is usually hardest when you are about to begin the process of living a minimalistic lifestyle. However, as time begins to pass and you keep up with what you have started, you will see that it will start getting better.

5. Declutter, please. The whole aim of the process was to get the things that are not needed away from your space, and that is what you need to start doing. This is where you begin to put in the physical work of clearing things away from your

environment. Be very honest with yourself as you do this. What are those things that you have very little or no need for? Please get them out of your space. You could give them out, or sell them at a thrift store, or do whatever it is you want with them. Remember, the goal is that they get away from your space after the process.

6. Apply this same process and the techniques that you have used when you are creating your to-do lists. Have this one thing at the back of your mind; your to-do list should contain the tasks that are only vital for you to accomplish that day. Do not clutter it with things that have no business being there. Doing this will only be anti-climactic and result in less productivity on your part.

7. Find the value in recycling and reusing things, in place of buying new ones every time. Recycling things is a great way to keep you from accumulating property again.

8. Find value in saving and investing your money in more profitable ventures. In all honesty, one of the major reasons why you end up spending so much on the things that you really do not need is because you have quite a lot of cash to spare after making your necessary expenditure. In order to make sure that you do not give in to the pressure that comes from having more money than you know what to do with it, turn to savings schemes and investment opportunities. This way, you would be forced to learn the value of financial intelligence. This is one thing that will help you as you journey on with your life.

Summary
Minimalism is a way of life that is quite handy as you journey towards increased productivity and getting more done. However, you must know that you will not achieve the state of living a minimalistic lifestyle from the first day you start trying. You will need to try and try again. So, in addition to all the things you have learned already, start forgiving yourself in advance.

You are definitely going to relapse into some old habits, but what matters is that you are able to detect when you are relapsing and that you are able to get yourself together in record time.

A Short message from the Author:

Hey, I hope you are enjoying the book? I would love to hear your thoughts!

Many readers do not know how hard reviews are to come by and how much they help an author.

I would be incredibly grateful if you could take just 60 seconds to write a short review on the product page of my book from where your purchased a copy, even if it is a few sentences!

Thanks for the time taken to share your thoughts!

Chapter 6

Get Rid of the Past and Bad Relationships

You must have heard this saying time and again; *you are a summary of the five people you spend most of your time with*. This statement goes to show you the value of relationships, and how you must make it a point of duty to guard your space jealously in terms of the people you allow to have access to you.

Despite this knowledge that the people in your life can make or mar you, quite a lot of people go ahead to accept negative people into their lives, and even when these people go away from their lives, they still remain hung up on them. If you are going to be as productive as you can get with your life, you must be able to understand that not all people should be with you. Consciously begin to sieve the people that have access to you, and most especially, *get rid of bad relationships*. In this chapter, we will be discussing some strategies you can adopt right now to get you the results you are looking for and step out from the shadows of the bad parts of your past.

Get Unstuck from Your Ugly Memories

Breathless gasps…

His hands fly frantically over the steering wheel as he tries to gain control of the car that has just slid off the road and is quickly tumbling down the hill.

He can feel his intestines as they clench in on one another, threatening to tear open and add to the pain he is going through…

Then the fires start. The smell of burning petrol, and the shouts of the lady seated next to him fill the air, piercing through his skin and feeling hotter and more painful that the fire he is in.

The pictures in his mind are vivid, clear and he can recall every detail as though it happened just a few minutes ago. It has been years since that experience that took the life of his beloved one, but he still wakes up every night with the screams resonating in his mind.

He jerks up immediately, covered in a cold sweat. He feels the despair as it rises up from within him – fresh and with a renewed vengeance. He may not be able to tell a lot, but he is certain that he may be living with those images for the rest of his life.

Fabian was in an accident a few years back, and in the process, he lost the one he was going to get married to. Although he survived, he is still not sure that it was a blessing because every night, he has battled with the same recurring dream that comes to haunt him.

His memories are too fresh, and he has been unable to get rid of them for good.

Our world today is filled with people who are battling with different memories from their past, and these memories in question are not good. In every direction you turn, you will most likely meet with someone that is battling some kind of trauma and gripping memories that haunt them from the past. One thing is common amongst these people; they usually wish that they can be free from the forces of the memories that jump at them. If you have the opportunity of meeting some of them at times when they are being plagued by these thoughts, you will discover that they are usually left weaker than they are and wishing that things can be different.

The ability to retain thoughts is a great ability bestowed upon man by nature. It is a great skill because it has heralded all the good things that have happened in the history of mankind. As a matter of fact, forgetfulness (especially in acute levels) is a medical issue and it usually calls for immediate medical attention because it is usually indicative of some form of deterioration in the brain and the person's cognitive functions.

As great as it is to be able to retain your memories, you would agree that there are some memories that you wish you could forget for good. A person who has been molested wishes that (s)he can forget about it and move on. A person who has been in an abusive relationship wishes that (s)he can forget it and move on. A child who grew up in the wrong kind of family would usually wish that (s)he can forget those formative years because of some of the experiences that he has had. The list is endless. There are a million things you wish you can press a *delete* button somewhere in your mind and forget about - automatically. However, you would agree that when it comes to these memories, they are quite difficult to let go of. This would usually be because of how deep they have been etched into your mind. However, in order to move forward, you must make a commitment to try; harder and smarter than you have tried before. This is a huge part of decluttering your mind, and it is vital that you do not skip this part.

Here are a few tips that can help you get unstuck from your bad memories.

1. The first step you should take is making the decision to forgive all those who have wronged

you, and do not exclude yourself while you do this. One of the reasons you still hurt this much and why the thoughts have refused to stop plaguing you is because you are yet to forgive the people who have wronged you. This is arguably the hardest part of the equation, but it is the most rewarding of all the steps you are to take, and it is what will give meaning to every other thing you will do in this regard.

Forgiving everyone who was involved in causing you pain is vital, but please do not forget to forgive yourself too. Many times, people go on to forgive everyone else, except themselves. As a result of this, they turn their anger inwards and start sabotaging themselves. This should not be the case.

You too, are worthy of being forgiven. Do not believe otherwise, and as a result of that, do all you can to let go.

2. Do not be afraid to let it all out. You cannot forgive yourself and others, and as a result, move on with your life and get unstuck from bad memories, if all you do is try to lock all you are feeling deep within you. It is not a bad idea to let the feelings out; cry if your must, bare your heart to someone if the need arises, just do anything that must be done to make sure that you do not hold it all back in. The danger of suppressing your feelings is that you will be tempted to turn it inwards, vent on those that come your way (who had nothing to do with what happened to you) or lose your cool sooner or later.

3. Commit to making good and new memories. Understand this; your mind cannot be empty, except there is a problem with it. It is your commitment to making new and very exciting memories that will make sure that those old and bad memories begin to fade away until they dissolve into nothingness. Hiding away in the darkness, and feeling sorry for yourself will only

make things worse. Go out, meet new people, make new friends, try new and exciting things. The aim is to make sure that you are not stuck in the cycle of your old memories for long.

4. Learn from the past, but please move on. Take the bad experiences you have had as teachers. A teacher comes to class because there is something that (s)he wants the students to learn from her/him. In the same way, know that the things that happened to you all have the capacity to teach you invaluable life lessons. So, while you make an effort to let go of the past, find the lessons and sieve them out of the experiences. Let go of the pain and the hurt that comes from having to experience such, but never the lessons you have learned.

5. Take some time off. There are times that the healing you need and the riddance to the memories of the past lie in as little as a time off your normal activities. This is the time you can spend to introspect and make resolutions for the

future. If you feel that it is a good thing to do and that it will contribute to the success of what you are up to, then by all means, please do that.

6. Depending on the severity of what happened, and the effects it is having on you right now, you may want to see a specialist. They are the ones with the skills, knowledge and experience that can be applied in real-time to be of help to you.

Let Go of Certain People

It is not news anymore that there are people that you should part ways with, especially as you are looking to declutter your life and become more productive with yourself. As you journey to becoming much better, here are a few people you must let go of.

1. Those that are not going your way. You have a vision and you are a man on an assignment. When you meet with people who behave as if

they don't have a vision, please do not be afraid to let them go.

2. Let go of those that do not have the same values as you do. There are people who do not hold in high esteem the things you do. All they will do is to weigh you down and make you feel as though you are wasting your time. Please, get them out of your circle.

3. Let go of those who are all for receiving from you but have nothing to give in exchange. There has to be something you stand to benefit from the relationship, and if there is nothing, please let them go.

4. Let go of those who are not intentional about seeing your value, understanding your worth and communicating to you that they value you. If they are constantly in the business of making you feel bad and inadequate for no reason, you need to begin to work on changing your circle.

5. Let go of those that surround you with negativity. These are the ones who never have anything positive to say – at all. They are all for the doom and gloom of life. You do not need those energies in your life, so let them go or they will make you start thinking and behaving like them.

6. Let go of those who are too self-centered. They believe the whole world revolves around them and they would do anything to keep the attention and spotlight on themselves. You don't need them around you.

Tips to Shake Off Bad Relationships from Your Life

The fact that you are trying to get specific people out of your life does not mean that you have to pick up a fight with them or become disrespectful. You know better, and there are ways to get the results you want to get without making it too obvious that that is what you are up to.

As we established at the beginning of this chapter, a bad relationship will be detrimental to you on all fronts. You must be trained to identify one, and on how to run as far away as you can from bad relationships. Here are a few pointers on how you know a bad relationship;

1. A terrible relationship leaves you drained each time. The other person in the relationship has all the characteristics of a leech/parasite, always looking for what to take from you and not what to give you in return. If you are the one doing most of the giving (of every kind), then you may want to take a step back.

2. There is little or no respect for boundaries. The other person does not understand what you mean when you say *don't do this*, or *I am not comfortable with that*. He intentionally chooses not to be interested in your decisions.

3. Unhealthy relationships are the ones in which the other party does not hesitate to remind you of your flaws and of the places that you are not so

good at. He does not do this with the attitude of love, but he does that in a bid to humiliate you and prevent you from aspiring for bigger things. You may also want to look out for relationships in which all that are discussed are bad things, gossip about others, bad news flying over the internet, and limiting conversations. In an unhealthy relationship, the other person never sees your value and is not intentional about communicating the beauty of your uniqueness to you.

4. An unhealthy relationship is one in which the other person is too controlling. They want to keep you on a short leash and tell you exactly what you must do.

5. The other person gets angry easily and may resort to abuse to get his points across. Abuse, in this context, does not only refer to physical beatings; emotional blackmail, psychological abuse and all the rest can be employed to get you to do the

things you are not willing and completely comfortable with doing.

Here are a few tips that can help you shake off bad relationships from your life.

1. Decide that you are going to end it and that you are not going to relapse into needing the attention and validation of that person. That is the first step you must take.

2. Make it official that you are taking a break. Let the person know that you will be unavoidably inaccessible to the person. You can decide to make a trip, spend some time alone, or do whatever that will take you away from the circumference of being around that person. As much as it lies within you, make this as long as it can safely be, and during this time, ensure that you are not in contact or any form of communication with him/ her.

3. Put structures in place to help you achieve this aim. It is not just enough to say that you want to stop a relationship. How do you want to achieve that? In this place, you need to begin to plan for what to do in cases of emergencies. Answer questions like *what do I do when/if this person decides to come see me? How do I explain away what I am doing so he/ she does not feel bad? How do I just avoid him/ her?*

   These structures will help you know how to go about it.

4. Start filling in the gaps immediately. The exit of people from your life will result in the opening of a gap from your life. It is your job to begin to fill up these gaps immediately. Get new friends who are more compatible with you and make sure that you start spending quality time with them. This way, you are beginning to close up the vacuum in your life, as well as sending sublime cues to the other person you are trying to get out of your life.

5. Stop trying to be friends. People can tell when you are trying so hard to be friends and bending over backward for them. If you are looking to nip that relationship in the bud, then stop trying so hard to be friends with them.

<u>Summary</u>

Your relationships matter so much as you journey toward productivity and decluttering your space to be more effective. Remember this, you are a summary of the five people you spend most of your time with, so make it a point of duty to sanitize your friends list on a regular basis.

While you are at it, please let go of the things that may have happened to you in the past. Learn from them, move on and decide not to be stuck in the past again. This is how you get to make use of the past as a ladder to step into the future.

Chapter 7

Pursue your Goals

There is every likelihood that you have heard about goal-setting before this time. As a matter of fact, goal-setting and the benefits of goal-setting have become a mantra on the lips of many people. Because of this heightened awareness, you receive after attending a class or seminar, you get back to your house and whisk out a sheet of paper.

On that piece of paper, you begin to write; you were told to make the goals big because the size of the goals would push you further and cause you to begin to strive harder. After a few long hours of writing and doing a lot of brain work, you take a look at the paper in hand – all the goals you want to accomplish within a time-frame have been written down there in black and white. Your heart is beating wildly and you are riding on the high of the dopamine and endorphins coursing through your veins. You feel optimistic, and there is this hope that you can wing it.

Fast forward to a few weeks later. You have lost the zeal you had a few weeks back. As a matter of fact, you cannot seem to find that book where you wrote down your goals anymore. For some reason, it seems to have vanished into thin air and to be very honest, you have not achieved up to 30% of the things you wrote down as goals – and the time is already far spent.

The real question is, why is this happening to you again? Why is it that even though you set goals, and do all that you have been taught to do, you still end up accomplishing a very little or insignificant part of what you wanted to achieve? One day you are up and pushing to go in the direction of achieving all your goals, the other day, you are down and completely out of it.

Why do you set goals that never get accomplished? In this chapter of the book, we will be taking a quick look at the above topic, and we will give you some ideas you can execute now in order to increase your productivity levels and begin to crush all your goals.

Discover Your Vocation

This may sound sad, but it is the truth. Many people feel uninspired and do not look forward to the next rising of the sun because, to be sincere, they have nothing to look forward to. Thee people are the ones who feel like they are observers; they are stuck in a life they do most want, married to the person they may not have wanted to marry in the first place, work a job they have no love for, and generally have to do things they do not want to do.

In this section of the book, however, we will be looking more at the job aspect [vocation]. Statistics have shown that the average person will spend a cumulative of 90,000 hours at his work, and this accounts for roughly one-third of his life. This is so for many people, but for others, it is not entirely so. The average entrepreneur/business owner will end up spending so much more than this as he journeys to the success of his venture over the course of his life. As a result of the amount of time that will finally go in to work over the course of your life, it is necessary that you pay attention to the nature of the work you spend your life on because this will play a very vital role as to how satisfied with life you will be, at the end of all things.

Inasmuch as many people have to work at a job (in most cases a nine-to-five, with the intentions of keeping themselves afloat and paying the bills), most of these people would soon get to a place where they would begin to feel that it has become vital for them to start looking for something else to get their hands on. This is where the concept of a vocation comes into place.

A vocation is an inclination to undertake a certain kind of work, especially a religious career, often in response to a perceived summoning or a higher call. Taking a look at this from a more sociological context, a vocation can be described to be a work you will do for the sake of doing it; you would do it, even if you are not paid to.

When you take a look at the definition above, you can see that the term *vocation* does not just talk about the job you were hired to do in your company and which you are paid to do. A vocation is that thing you are passionate about, and which you have started executing on, that you do not mind doing even when you are not paid. It could be your job, a passion you have or come from a skill you have picked up along the way.

If you are going to be productive and get to accomplish all the things you have set out to accomplish, you must be intentional about finding out whatever your vocation is. The reason for this is the fact that your vocation comes with a passion/zeal/drive that is independent of the salary you are paid. Because it is something you love to do naturally, you will not have to deal with the overwhelming desire to quit or the problems that accompany not being driven.

This is one way to make sure that you are always motivated to get on with the things you must do; find and channel your concentration toward your vocation, and you will be surprised at the amount of success you will record and the results you will see.

To discover your vocation, these are a few tips that can help you.

1. Your vocation usually lies in and is connected to the gifts you have within you. So, in order to get started with finding it, you may want to start by making a list of the inert abilities and talents you have.

2. The next thing you need to look at is passion. Out of all the gifts you have within, which of them are you most passionate about. This could be an indication as to what direction you should be headed to.

3. Another thing you need to consider is the money factor. What are the things you will do even if money were not to be a factor in the equation? If

you were not paid, what are the things you would do?

4. Remember to listen. The art of finding your vocation and the call of your main life's assignment will not come when you are not listening. You must listen; to the voice of your inner self (through mindfulness, introspection and meditation). Also, listen to what people that really know you say to you; those could be invaluable cues you do not want to miss out on.

What Motivates You? – Your Passions

We cannot skip this without talking in-depth about your passions. Having a clear understanding of your passions can be the difference between success and failure.

One of the major reasons why you may struggle with productivity, meeting your goals and being able to do the things you should be doing may be because, in the maze of all the activities you are trying to carry out, there is really nothing you are passionate about in there. When you keep trying to go at something you are not passionate about (at all), there is every chance that you will keep struggling to achieve it. The result of this struggle will be that you will not be able to achieve all that you set to do and over a period of time, you may begin to feel as though you are a loser. This can eventually take a toll on your self-esteem, and the rest is history.

In order to prevent this cascade of activities, it is vital that you have a clear understanding of what your passions are. You need to be able to tune inwards, ask and answer a few questions very critically. Here are a few of those questions you should begin to ask if you want to find your passion.

1. If you could only do one thing today, what would that one thing be?

2. What do you REALLY want out of your life?

3. What makes you extremely happy, even if doing it will mean that you will have to let go of some other 'equally' important things?

4. What is the thing you would gladly do and keep doing even if no one sees you to commend you and you are not paid to do it?

5. /What riles you up and makes you wish that you had what it takes to correct it immediately?

6. If all your problems were solved now, what would you still do with all the time you would have on your hands?

These questions, and more, will give you some insight into what your passion really is.

The Goals That Work - S M A R T Goals

Now that you have clearer knowledge about what your vocation is, your passion and how you can tell what your passions truly are, it is time for us to take a closer look at your goals once again. Take a look at this section of the chapter from the lens of the knowledge you have been able to gather in the preceding lines, and the knowledge you have now gotten by answering the questions above.

You may have heard of this before now, the concept of SMART goals. Let us take a look at what this means and how it affects you as a person who is on the way to becoming more productive.

SMART is an acronym given to serve as a guide when creating your goals and setting objectives. Experts and those that have made use of this template over time have agreed that this is one template that guarantees that your goals get met and that you commit to the process of doing so. So, here's a quick breakdown of the SMART goals.

S – Your goals must be Specific. This is because if you are not able to articulate (in very clear and concise terms) what you want to achieve, there is every tendency that you will end up not getting much done – even after working for a very long season. For example, I want to make XYZ amount of money.

M – Your goal must be Measurable. How will you know that you are making progress toward the actualization of the goal that you have set for yourself? There must be indices that you will make use of to signify your progress. For example, to achieve the goal of making XYZ amount of money, there are activities that will signify that you are on the right track. Could it be getting more leads for your business? Getting past clients to purchase from you again? Name them.

A – Your goal must be Attainable/Achievable. Your mind must be able to perceive the goal as something that you can do. If this does not happen, you will NOT achieve the goal. This is what will make sure that you keep at it, even when you see a million reasons to give up and throw in the towel.

R -Your little goal must be Relevant. With respect to the achievement of a bigger purpose/target, what you are doing now - the goal you want to commit to must be relevant. If your goals are not relevant, there would be no drive to push on with them, especially as the days unfold. For example, in a corporate setting, the goals of a unit or department must be relevant to the overall goals of the organization.

T – Your goals must be Time-bound. Over the years, it has been said that a goal without a time-frame is a mere wish. One of the most-potent inspirations to put in the work required to achieve something is the threat of a looming deadline. So, the next time you want to set a goal, include a realistic timeline. For example, I want to make XYZ amount of money within the *next three months*.

Include all these features in your next goal-setting episode, and you would see a difference.

How to Set SMART Goals That WORKS!

Now that you have understood the concept of goal-setting, and the features that make a goal to have a higher chance of getting achieved, it is time you learned how to set SMART goals, and position for these goals to be achieved.

Here are a few practical steps to help you achieve this aim.

1. Define clearly WHY you need to achieve the goal. After you have set the goal you want to achieve, the next thing you must do is state why you must achieve it. This will make sure that you commit to the process and see things through till the end.

2. Be clear about all the parameters that should be captured in the goal-setting exercise. The SMART aspects of the goal must be clear enough.

3. Gather all the tools and resources you will need to actualize the goal you have set. Human

resources, materials, trainings and equipments; make sure that you have all of them.

4. Set KPIs. Key Performance Indicators are like the checkpoints in your journey to achieving the goal you have set for yourself. They are those factors that validate that you are on the right track, like the mini-wins that will take you to the ultimate win you have in mind. When you are done with setting your goal, be clear about your KPIs.

5. Do not trivialize the place of accountability. We've spoken extensively about getting accountability partners to help you on your journey, make sure you get that done.

6. Connect your goals to your passions. This is the reason why we had to start by laying the foundation of explaining what passions are and how you can discover your passions. Now that you have set your goals, make sure that they revolve around something that you are passionate about. Your passions are what will

keep you striving towards the actualization of your goals and make you see challenges as setbacks and not defeat.

Summary

To be able to be as productive as you truly want to be, you must make a commitment to discover your vocation, pinpoint your passions and the things you really love to do, and set goals that are SMART. When you have set your goals, connect them to your passions and keep at it; that is the way you can achieve even the most difficult of goals.

Chapter 8

Practice Mindfulness

We live in a world that is full of noise and in every direction you turn, there are distractions trying to pull you away from the things you should give attention to. According to a study carried out and pioneered by Microsoft, the average person in today's world has an attention span of only eight seconds. This means that under normal circumstances, you can only hold down and keep the attention of a regular person for only 8 seconds before he is off to do the next best thing that catches his fancy.

Considering this, and the fact that we spoke about finding your vocation (which is a very difficult thing to do), it becomes increasingly difficult for people to be able to achieve their goal of finding their vocation/connecting with a higher sense of purpose.

How do you connect with a higher sense of purpose when you cannot even seem to hear your own voice again – because it has been overwhelmed by the noise in today's world.

How do you find your true calling and know for sure what you are called to do when you cannot tune inwards and listen to yourself for once?

These and more become the problems that you face today. Expectations are high on you, so you feel constrained towards following a path that has been carved out by friends and well-meaning family members. There is the pressure to be exact and precise in all you do, so you are afraid to even try for the sake of the fact that whatever you try may fail, and you would have to start from ground zero again. Until you learn how to shut the external noise outside of you and look inwards, you won't be able to find a lot of the heavier answers in life that you are looking for. That is why this chapter has been created; to show you exactly how you can shut out all the noise and focus on finding the things that really matter to you.

What is Mindfulness?

As you may be able to tell by now, mindfulness is a state of heightened awareness that is usually brought about by a season of intentionally exposing yourself to be highly attentive to the forces of the Universe. Mindfulness is a sense of total calm and quietness, achieved as a result of completely focusing one's attention on the present and letting go of the past or the future, and is usually carried out as a therapeutic process, or in pursuit of something more valuable (like the answers to some real questions).

All the people you know who have come to accomplish great feats in this world were those who did not play with the practice of mindfulness. To different people, it may have come using different ways and through different means, but it all boils down to the same fact that at some point in their lives, they had to let go of everything and just open themselves up to the power that comes from within.

Why You Need to Practice Mindfulness

As stated in the last section, mindfulness is a very vital part of every outstanding success story. Here are a few reasons why you should start practicing mindfulness;

1. At the back of every notable achievement and sustainable success was the conscious opening of the mind to something more divine. Mindfulness is the process through which this opening can happen.

2. It helps you cut out unnecessary distractions and noise, and helps you learn how to begin to look within for solutions to your problems while at it.

3. The practice of mindfulness can help you reduce stress. Since you are consciously choosing to let go of every memory and just focus on the now, you will also let go of all the stress that comes

with memories. This is one of the major reasons why it is used as a therapeutic measure.

4. Mindfulness helps make you more aware of your emotions, and as a result of this, you are equipped to become a better person and as a result, have better relationships.

5. Mindfulness is a major tool that can help you achieve mental, emotional, physical, and cognitive balance and mastery in a short time. This tool helps you train almost all aspects of your well-being at the same time, and this is why practices like yoga are founded upon it.

Effective Techniques for Practicing Mindfulness

As indicated in the section above, mindfulness does not come in only one form. Consider it to be a faculty in a college, with all the departments that fall under it. There are a lot of ways through which you can practice mindfulness, but all of them lead to the same results.

Mindful Meditation

Mindful meditation is more than just thinking. It involves meditating and fixating on the thoughts that flit through your mind, without thinking of them in terms of being good or bad or trying to analyze a lot of them. Mindful meditation pursues a state of sereneness and complete attention on the now. Here's how you carry out mindful meditation.

1. Sit relaxed. In most cases, it is advisable that you stay in an upward posture with your back straight.

2. Make sure your physical environment is clean. Take away anything that can confuse or distract you from what you want to do.

3. Make sure the place is quiet and if there must be noise, make sure that they are smooth songs that can aid meditation. Focus on your breathing and on a mantra, which you will be repeating again and again – under your breath. Focus on these

things till every other thing begins to fade away and your thoughts are only about what should be at the fore of your mind at the moment.

4. Notice body sensations, the random thoughts that cross your mind, feelings and emotions, and every other thing in-between. At this point, you are more attuned to feeling and you will see that you will start seeing things in greater depth.

5. At this point, you become more open to ideas, plans and thoughts begin to swarm your head. Take note of them, and begin to take action immediately.

Mindful Observation

This is the practice of taking a closer look at things (people, events, activities, places, etc.), with the sole intent of seeing things that are not easily seen by others and observing the connection between seemingly disconnected events.

To carry out mindful observation requires extreme attention to detail. It pays that you just block out distractions and focus on the thing you want to look at. With your eyes on it, begin to look at the characteristics of the object or study the details of the event. If your mind is to wander away, bring it back and continue the task at hand.

The aim of this is to be able to learn as much as you can about whatever you are observing and to be able to establish a connection between it and yourself so that you can go on to replicate some results.

Mindful Listening and Breathing

Mindful listening is a communication tool that differentiates expert communicators from the mediocre ones. It is the practice of listening to someone without judging him, interrupting him, to allowing the feelings of disagreement to come in the way of what the person is saying. It is the process of blocking out everything else, with the intent to hear someone (both what he is saying and what he is not saying), pick out the cues that are right before you, and generally contribute to making his life easier.

To be a better mindful listener,

1. Set it as a target. Many people do not see the need to do this, and their relationships with people take the back seat as a result of the fact that they are not good listeners.

2. Understand that it is bound to happen. Notwithstanding how much good intents you may have, there is bound to be those few seconds when you get wrapped up in your own thoughts as the person is speaking to you, or your mind tends to wander. Don't beat yourself up unnecessarily, it will only reduce as time passes and you train yourself the more.

3. When you notice your mind wandering, carefully bring it back. The goal of doing this is to make sure that the person does not notice that you

spaced out in the middle of a conversation; that can give someone's ego a real beating.

4. Keep up with this process until you have mastered the art of mindful listening. When you get to this point, one of the major effects is that people will be inclined to conversing with you because they will see you as someone worth talking to.

Mindful breathing is the act of focusing your attention on your breathing, with the intent of taking better breaths or just to focus more on the now. This is a great therapeutic tool and can come in handy to help you control your emotions – especially those of anger and worry.

To carry this out,

1. Be in a comfortable position; lying, sitting or standing – it is up to you.

2. Focus on the breaths as they come in and go out of your body. As you inhale, feel the air as it comes into your lungs, and do the same while you exhale. The result of this is that within a few minutes, you will get complete control over yourself, and the aim for which you have done the exercise would have been achieved. This is also necessary and can come in handy when you are looking to carry out a full body scan on yourself. As the feelings intensify, you can then tune inwards and begin to look out for the things that do not feel right in your body.

Guided Meditation

Guided meditation is the practice of meditation, but the only major difference is that this is carried out under the supervision of a coach or someone who will focus on walking you through the process. It is basically the process of letting someone who is skilled in the act take you through while you follow his instructions and get on with the things he asks you to do.

There are various sources of guided meditations, including:

1. Apps such as Mindfulness Training, Headspace, and Simply Being

2. Podcasts such as The daily meditation podcast with Mary Meckley, 10% happier with Dan Harris, and The Meditation Oasis.

Reflect on Your Thoughts

This is one thing you should be doing as you engage in almost all of your mindfulness exercises. When you carry out mindful observation, breathing and mindful meditation, one of the major things you should be doing is making sure that you are focused on your thoughts. This is one way you can take control of your thinking pattern and make the most of every moment.

To achieve this, in the height of your mindfulness exercise, focus on the thoughts that pass through your mind. Remember that the aim is to keep track and not be judgemental. So be conscious and open to receiving new ideas as you reflect on your thoughts. If, in the event, you notice bad thoughts trying to make an appearance, focus on clearing them from your mind immediately.

Self-Compassion Breaks

Self-compassion breaks are practices you can engage in at any time of the day. They are known to be short (so you do not need a lot of time), and relatively easy to follow. The goal of carrying out this exercise is to see to it that you can get out of a stressful situation or release a reasonable amount of self-compassion whenever it is needed. Here are the steps you should follow;

1. Remember to be in a comfortable position. Call a stressful situation to mind. Take a look at it critically; can you feel the stress and pain that comes with remembering it?

2. If yes, then you will need to make use of affirmations. Acknowledge the moment of

suffering by saying something along the lines of *this is a moment of suffering*. This a form of mindfulness, and once you have admitted that there is a problem, you can commit to fixing it. Next, you want to remind yourself that life is not a bed of roses and that challenges come everyone's way. This serves as a common denominator and makes sure that you do not end up isolating yourself and feeling worse than you probably should.

3. At this point, make a resolution to be kind to yourself. Say this out loud so that you can hear it; *I will be kind to myself.* Make use of any phrase that comes to you naturally, but be sure that you are not missing out on the goal of the exercise – which is to release some kindness for yourself. You may also want to make use of statements like; *I accept myself! I forgive myself! I move on from this*, and so on.

Summary

Mindfulness is a major part of every successful man's success. You must be able to let go of the past and focus on the present moment. This is the only way through which you can open your mind up to new ideas, unleash your inner genius, and be sure to rise above feelings of depression.

Mindfulness comes in various forms. Find out the one you can practice at every time and make use of it, but be sure that you are mixing all of them up as you journey towards getting more productive at every point and decluttering your mind from overthinking.

Chapter 9

Be Happy

We have spoken extensively about your productivity. In the pages of this book, we have discussed strategies you can employ now if you are looking to achieve more with your life and your time, become the person you have envisioned yourself to be and generally bring on your A-game at every point. However, if we do not take out a little time to stress the value of happiness and why you should prioritize it, you will become the person you have always wanted to be, but the only exception will be that you will not be as happy as you should be.

Happiness is a physical/emotional state that you should not compromise or trade for anything at any point. If you have paid close attention this far, you should have noticed that the reason we have discussed all we have is because of the importance of higher productivity and achieving more on your happiness. There is a sense of happiness that comes with knowing that you are productive with your time, affecting lives while you are at it, and being at your best in every situation. In this section of the book, we will take a quick look at a few things you must have in mind if you will be as happy as you should always be at every point. Add these tips to your to-do list and watch your happiness as it skyrockets.

Live Your Best Life

This is something you must commit to having at the back of your mind at every time; the knowledge and intentions of living your best life at every point. As we stressed in the section of this book where we spoke about the art of mindfulness, the only guaranteed span of time you have is the now, and what you do with it/how you make use of it matters a lot and will go a great way to making sure that you get to the place of satisfaction and fulfillment.

Living your best life entails that you take note of, and keep to practicing the following;

1. Giving up on procrastination and beginning to live the dreams you have for yourself – right from this moment.

2. Forgiving yourself and others that may have wronged you in the past. This is the only way that you can be sure that you will be free of anger.

3. Living a balanced life; the kind of life in which one aspect is not exalted to a point where it outweighs the other aspects of your life.

4. Doing the things that make you happy, as far as no one gets hurt and you don't get in the way of other people by doing so.

5. Having a commitment to growth, to become better than the person you were a second ago, and keep to growing/evolving as you take the next steps forward and journey towards becoming a person of more relevance.

Steps You Can Take to be Happy

Here are a few things you can do in order to be truly happy;

1. You must understand that when it comes to happiness, there is really not a one-size-fits-all approach to it. You must be able to clearly define what makes you happy and commit to doing these things even when you think they are unnecessary. All you will find in books and journals are ideas, and you should not limit the scope of your experimenting to the ideas you will find in these books.

2. Begin each day with a list of things you are truly grateful for, and your affirmations for the day. This will give you a head start for the day.

3. Give compliments, and be open to receiving them when they come your way. Do over with unnecessary cynicism and trying to read a lot of

meaning into everything people say to you, even when what they say are good things.

4. Learn to give people the benefit of the doubt, and also make excuses for them. This allows you to have peace with yourself and focus your energies on the things that really matter to you.

5. Consciously walk away from fights, unnecessary arguments and squabbling, even when you are going to be seen as a weakling or a person that is not strong enough to hold his own. There are some points that you do not need to prove. If you must, allow the powers above you to handle discrepancies that seem to be persistent.

6. Exercise your body and your mind as well. This helps keep the blood pumping and makes sure that you are at a place of peak performance.

7. Do not joke with your "me" time. This is the time you spend alone, doing one thing that makes you feel really good. It entails consciously shutting

out from the bustle that is associated with life and of the days and chasing after little luxuries like having a cup of your favorite chocolate, spending time with your loved ones, and indulging your favorite show.

8. Consciously work on doing away with bad habits and taking up good and new ones. This helps with your sense of self-control and your self-esteem in general. While you are at it, work on perfecting your people skills; you won't be an island, so it is best you prepare yourself for the inevitable meeting with humans.

Summary

Your happiness is just as necessary as all the things we have discussed in earlier parts of this book. Do not be caught up in the rush that is called the world of today, such that you put yourself and your happiness at the tail end of the equation. Rather, actively seek out the things that make you feel good, and learn to include them in your everyday to-do lists.

The end... almost!

Hey! We've made it to the final chapter of this book, and I hope you've enjoyed it so far.

If you have not done so yet, I would be incredibly thankful if you could take just a minute to leave a quick review on my book product page.

I would be incredibly grateful if you could take just 60 seconds to write a short review on the product page of my book from where your purchased a copy, even if it is a few sentences!

Even if it is just a sentence or two!

So if you really enjoyed this book, please...

Leave a brief review on on the product page of my book from where your purchased a copy.

I truly appreciate your effort to leave your review, as it truly makes a huge difference.

Chapter 10

Reach Out to Someone

This is one mistake that many people make; they believe that they are enough, and this prevents them from timely seeking to reach out to and connect with people.

Do not take the phrase – you are enough – to mean that you are an island that can exist on your own. Our world is wired to be heavily interconnected, and there is no way you can escape this fact. As a result of this, it is vital that you learn how to forge connections with people.

On your journey to becoming more relevant, more productive, and achieving a whole lot more with your life, if you ever get to the place where you feel as though you are stuck and not sure about the next step you must take, make it a point of duty to seek for help from other people. There are those who are more equipped to be of help to you at these points, reach out to them, and seek to connect with them.

DO NOT BE AFRAID TO ASK FOR HELP and no, it does not make you weak. As a matter of fact, the fact that you reach out to someone for help is a sign of strength; it implies that you have identified that you are not able to help yourself in an area and that you are willing to let someone else be of help to you in that place.

These people could be friends, colleagues, family, acquaintances, and every other person in-between. The aim is to reach out to them as the need arises so that you do not feel alone and face the problems you are battling with on your own. There is always someone nearby – willing and able to help. Find them and reach out to them.

Get Professional Help If All Else Fails

Inasmuch as this is a self-help book, it does not, in any way seek to replace the role of the professionals in your life. If you have tried all that has been discussed in this book and you are still having challenges, it is very wise that you reach out to a professional and get help from him on a more professional level.

Depending on the nature of the challenge you may have, find out the professionals that are equipped to handle those kinds of challenges and reach out to them for help. This is one way to know for sure what may be the problem and get started with solving it.

Professionals have your best interest at heart, make great use of them.

Conclusion

Within the pages of this book, we have examined in detail the concept of overthinking and why you may be fighting with this at every point in your life. We have discussed the causes of this, the effects and why you must commit to changing the narrative. As said, you will not be able to accomplish anything worthwhile if you allow overthinking rob you of everything you can do, and prevent you from reaching out into the future that you want to step into.

We have also discussed proven strategies that you can employ right now in order to see to it that you stop overthinking things and that in place of doing this, you become the person that does more of action. The steps that have been discussed so far are actionable, simple and concise. They were delivered in this format to ensure that you are able to see where you fit into the scheme of things and make sure that you begin to take action on all that you have learned immediately.

That is what you need to do right now; take action. Get a piece of paper and answer these questions right now.

Now that I have read this book till this point, what one step do I need to take to make sure that I begin to make the most out of all that I have learned? After taking that one step, what is the next step? And the next?

Now that you know exactly where to start, start immediately.

Remember, it is insanity to do the same thing over and again, and expect different results while doing the same thing you have been doing. Nothing works that way.

References

The following online resources have been consulted with and cited at different sections of this book.

Morin, A. April 2017. Science says this is what happens to you when you over think everything. Retrieved from https://www.inc.com/amy-morin/science-says-this-is-what-happens-when-you-overthink-things.html

Cherney, K. March 2020. Effects of Anxiety on the body. Retrieved from https://www.healthline.com/health/anxiety/effects-on-body#1

Abhyuday-Tiwari. April 2019. What is overthinking? What are the causes of overthinking? Retrieved from https://www.thenationaltv.com/Article/what-is-overthinking-what-are-the-causes-of-overthinking

Aman, J.L. July 2013. Five reasons fear journals benefit mental health. Retrieved from https://www.healthyplace.com/blogs/anxiety-schmanxiety/2013/07/five-reasons-you-should-keep-a-fear-journal

Kiander, T. February 2020. How to create a to=do list that super boosts your productivity. Retrieved from https://www.lifehack.org/articles/productivity/how-to-create-a-to-do-list-that-makes-you-smile.html

Becomingminimalist.com. N.d. Benefits of minimalism; 21 benefits of owning less. Retrieved from https://www.becomingminimalist.com/minimalism-benefits/

McKay, K., McKay, B. June 2010. Finding your calling part IV: Discovering your vocation. Retrieved from https://www.artofmanliness.com/articles/finding-your-calling-part-iv-discovering-your-vocation/

Usiagwu, M. July 2019. 5 major reasons why you need to practice mindfulness; Importance of mindfulness. Retrieved from https://thriveglobal.com/stories/5-major-reasons-why-you-need-to-practice-mindfulness/

CFI. N.d. SMART goal. Retrieved from https://corporatefinanceinstitute.com/resources/knowledge/other/smart-goal/

www.ingramcontent.com/pod-product-compliance
Lightning Source LLC
Chambersburg PA
CBHW050321120526
44592CB00014B/2004